Roll

RICK HANSEN

WHEELS AROUND

THE WORLD

Ainslie Manson
ILLUSTRATED BY Ron Lightburn

On

GREYSTONE BOOKS

Vancouver/Berkeley

Jack was thrilled when Rick Hansen visited him in the hospital. He was Jack's hero.

Rick had been thrown from the back of a truck when he was just a little older than Jack. His injury hadn't slowed him down for long. Soon he was playing wheelchair basketball and racing in wheelchair marathons.

Rick made Jack laugh by doing a
wheelie right beside his bed.

"Learn to look forward, not back," Rick
told Jack. "Get up and start wheeling."

And that's exactly what Jack did.

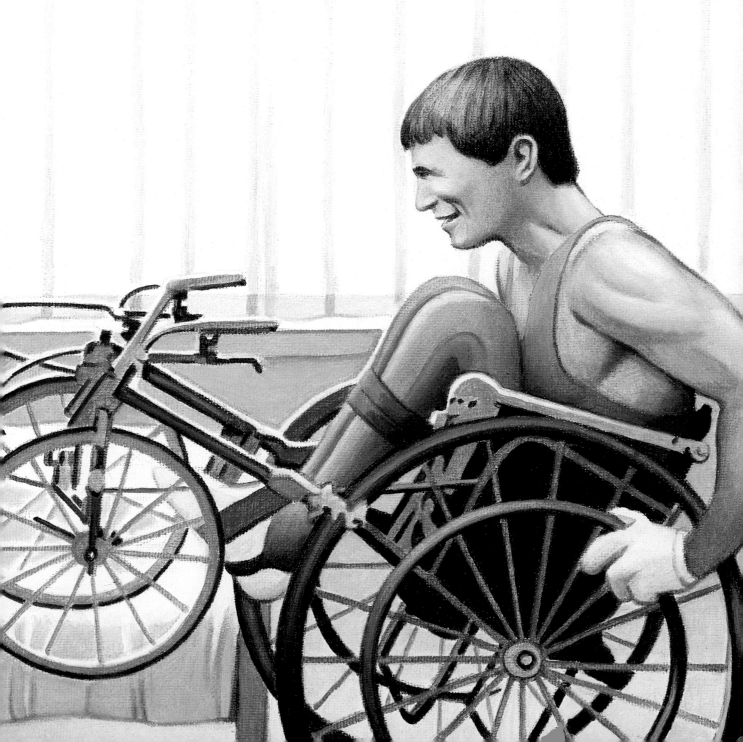

Vancouver, B.C. | *March 21, 1985*

Today Jack's hero was taking on a new challenge. Rick was going to wheel around the world.

"Come on," Jack called to his sister. "We don't want to be late. Rick Hansen's Man in Motion World Tour is about to begin!"

Jack had the perfect viewing spot. Then a big man with a big camera stepped right in front of him.

"You're blocking my view," said Jack. He meant to give the man a gentle nudge, but someone bumped him from behind.

"Hey," said the man, nearly dropping his camera, "I'm taking pictures for the newspaper!"

"But I can't see Rick," Jack complained.

Jack twisted to the left. He twisted to the right. Finally, a tiny space opened up, and there Rick was.

"Bon voyage!" Jack shouted.

Rick planned to wheel sixty to eighty kilometres every day for the next two years. Jack was exhausted from wheeling just ten blocks to see him off!

Roll on, roll on,
Push, push, push,
Cross the first border,
And wheel all the way across the USA

Rick's shoulders ached, and his hands were blistered.
He had wheeled over mountains and across deserts.
Often the road seemed long and lonely. But as he
neared the coast in Florida, he saw children up ahead.

Beth's friend Sandy tapped her on the arm and pointed.
   "Yes, here he comes!" said Beth.
   Like Rick, Sandy was a paraplegic, paralyzed from
the waist down. But Sandy had trouble
speaking, too.
   Sandy handed Rick a picture she had drawn. It
showed Rick wheeling across a finish line.
   "You're an incredible artist," Rick said.
   "She's the greatest," said Beth. But Beth knew
Sandy couldn't take art at school because the art
room was up three flights of stairs. Beth had an idea.
Hey, they should move the art room to the ground
floor. Yes! She'd talk to the principal this afternoon.

Roll on, roll on,
Push, push, push,
Ireland, Scotland, ENGLAND

Not only did Rick have the flu, but they had made a wrong turn. And now a bus was honking at them to get out of the way!

The sisters stepped off the bus and found themselves face-to-face with Rick Hansen.

"We heard about you in school today," said Hannah.

"And here I am," said Rick, "lost, in the middle of London."

"I'll get help," said Holly.

Hannah tried not to stare. Rick looked terrible. "You've wheeled all the way from Canada?"

"Not across the ocean," said Rick. "My wheelchair doesn't have wings!"

"But you look so tired. Are you feeling ill?"

Rick nodded.

"Would you like a lemon drop? Or my clean hankie?"

Holly returned before Rick could answer. "They're sending the Queen's own motorcycle escort to show you the way."

"Here they come!" said Hannah.

"You girls are amazing," said Rick. "I feel better already."

"He does look green!" said Holly, as Rick waved and wheeled on.

"Even famous people get the flu," said Hannah.

Roll on, roll on,
Push, push, push,
France, Belgium, Holland, Germany, Denmark,
Norway, Sweden, Finland, Russia, and POLAND

Rick tried to ignore his problems and think about one day at a time. They'd had trouble with his chair, with the motor home, with team members. And now—did he smell smoke? Was someone yelling?

"Fire! Help!" Patryk shouted in Polish. He had walked past the motor home, hoping to catch a glimpse of Rick Hansen. Instead, he saw smoke billowing from a window.

Two members of the team rushed inside and carried Rick out, then rushed back in again.

Patryk realized Rick had been rescued in such a hurry, he hadn't had time to pull on his trousers. Rick noticed too, and they both burst out laughing.

As soon as it was safe, Patryk went inside and found the missing trousers and brought Rick his wheelchair.

"Thank you for your help," Rick said.

Patryk didn't understand his English words, but Rick's grateful expression and handshake said it all.

That night a special reception was being held in Rick's honour. Patryk ran home to get ready.

Roll on, roll on,
Push, push, push,
Czech Republic, Austria, Switzerland,
Spain, Portugal, Morocco, and ITALY

Rick was exhausted when he crossed the border into Italy.
But it would be midnight before he got to bed. And he'd still
have to be up at 5:30. His whole team was grumbling—but
especially the two men on laundry duty.

Matteo had come to the laundromat with his grandmother's
laundry—and his cousin Gianna. She was visiting from
Canada, and she was blind.

    Two men were joking in English as they emptied a dryer.

    "You're part of the Man in Motion World Tour," said Gianna.

    Matteo watched in horror as she sat down to chat—on
their laundry! A T-shirt stuck to her leg.

    "Yuck," Gianna said, "it's sticky!"

    "We put tar on Rick's gloves to make gripping easier,"
said one of the men. "It gets on everything."

    "Try getting it off with ice," said Gianna.

    "Good idea," said the other man. "We will."

    When the men had left, Gianna told Matteo about
Rick. "He wants to make life easier for everyone with
disabilities," she said.

    "Even people who sit on his laundry?"
Matteo teased.

    Gianna laughed. "Absolutely!"

Roll on, roll on,
Push, push, push,
Serbia, Croatia, Greece, Bahrain,
Then JORDAN *and* ISRAEL

Rick rolled onto the bridge. It was small but well guarded. It was the only connection between Israel and Jordan. Near the middle, four children were waiting to speak with him.

Hessa and Adiva were from Jordan. Levi and Eli
were from Israel. Their countries did not get along.

"Here he comes!" said Hessa.

"Are the four of you part of a team?" Rick asked,
shaking hands with each of them.

"Kind of," Eli said. "We belong to a friendship
club for kids from our two countries."

"Trying to work together isn't always easy,"
said Adiva.

"I'm sure it's not," said Rick. "I bet you really
have to listen to each other."

"We do," said Levi. "But it's worth it."

Roll on, roll on,
Push, push, push,
To NEW ZEALAND

Even though they had a flowering plant to serve as a
Christmas tree, Rick was homesick. He was glad when
Christmas was over and he was back on the road.

Rowan and Connor were ready and waiting. When
Rick and a friend wheeled into sight, the boys shot
out of the bush.

"Can we join you?" Connor asked.

Rick grinned. "Come on," he said.

The boys told Rick that because of him, they had
joined a wheelchair sports team and were training
for competitions.

Rick told them stories about the countries he'd
visited and how kind everyone had been. "But in many
places," he said, "so much still has to be done to make
it easier to get around in a wheelchair."

"Like ramps into buildings," said Rowan.

"You got it," said Rick.

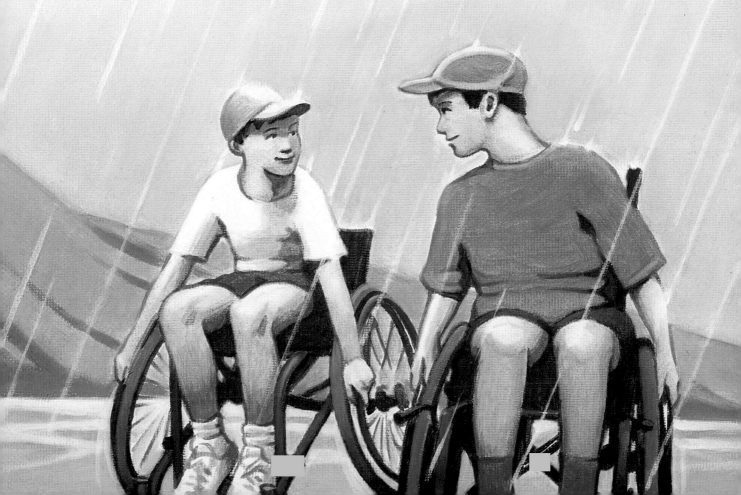

Roll on, roll on,
Push, push, push
To AUSTRALIA

Halfway around the world! Rick had managed one half.
He was ready for the other. But before he rolled on, he
had questions to answer.

A group of schoolchildren had gathered to meet him.
    "Today," Rick told them, "a team member sprayed
a halfway line on the highway with whipped cream,
and I burst through it."

"Yum!" a boy shouted.

The kids laughed.

"Do you get lonely on the road all by yourself?" asked a girl.

Rick gestured to his team. "They're always with me. Often they jog or bike beside me, and the motor home is right behind."

"Aren't you afraid they'll run you down?" another boy asked.

"Never," said Rick. "They're extra careful."

"Do you ever feel like quitting?"

"No," said Rick. "But sometimes when I'm hurting, tired, or discouraged, I have to wheel away the 'grumps,' so I don't take it out on my team members."

"Will you be home soon?" a little girl asked.

"Not soon," said Rick. "But I'm halfway there!"

Roll on, roll on,
Push, push, push,
To Hong Kong and CHINA

This was the day Rick had been dreaming about.
Climbing the Great Wall of China was going to
be incredibly hard work. But if he didn't begin, he
couldn't finish. At the very highest point, a little
girl was watching him.

Lin had been chosen to congratulate Rick when
he reached the summit. They clinked cups of tea
in a toast to Rick's success.

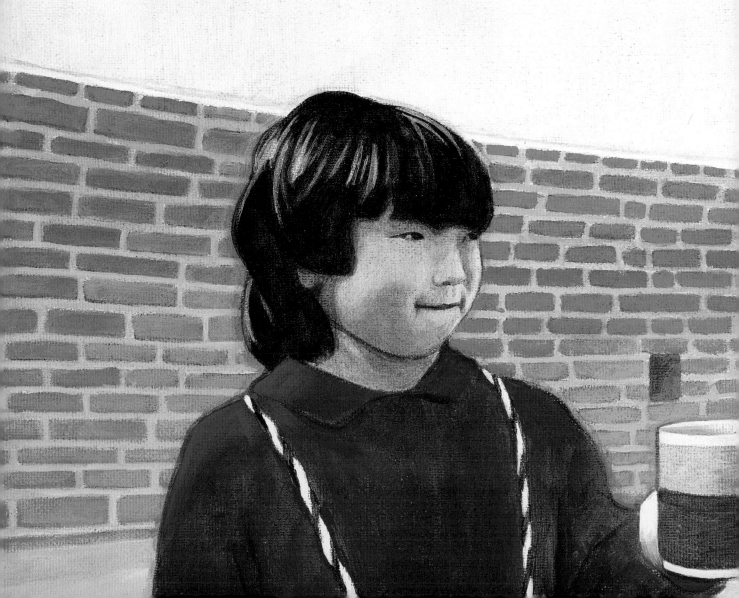

Through an interpreter, Rick said he liked Lin's red dress. He also said, "There are no walls in life you can't climb. There is nothing you can't do if you set your mind to it."

Lin dreamed of being a ballerina. It was very hard, though, to practise when she wanted to play outside.

As Rick wheeled on, Lin pictured herself on stage, leaping gracefully over a wall as high as the Great Wall of China.

Roll on, roll on,
Push, push, push,
Korea, Japan, back to the USA,
Then home to CANADA

Cape Spear, Newfoundland! Rick still had the whole country to cross, but he was back in Canada. With a smile on his face, he began wheeling west. A girl on a bike followed.

Leslie climbed off her bike to talk to a team member. "Excuse me," she said. "Rick is passing by so quickly, people don't realize he's accepting donations for spinal cord research. I could help."

The next day Leslie returned with two ice cream buckets and a *Donations* sign attached to her bike.

Soon she was tapping on the motor home window. "Could you carry this, please? It weighs a ton!"

Her backpack was full of money. The buckets had filled so fast, she'd had to keep emptying them. By the end of the day, she had collected almost five thousand dollars.

"Way to go, Leslie!" said Rick. "Come join my birthday party."

The table was piled high with food from thoughtful Newfoundlanders—including seven birthday cakes. Leslie ate until she was ready to burst.

Roll on, roll on,
Push, push, push,
Across TEN PROVINCES

Although Rick had wheeled three-quarters of the way
around the world, he knew the toughest part of the tour
still lay ahead. He couldn't relax, not for a minute, not yet!

Everyone along the way seemed to know about Rick.
Canadians were welcoming him home and cheering him on.
　　In town after town in the Maritimes, he was treated
like a rock star.

Autumn arrived, and Rick wheeled under brilliantly coloured trees in Quebec.

In Ontario, the Prime Minister presented him with a cheque for a million dollars!

Rick reached the Prairies in the middle of winter. He wore a computerized snowsuit that had been invented especially for him. Sensors warned when his body was too cold and it was time to go inside and warm up.

In Alberta, First Nations elders gave Rick an eagle feather. "For strength," they said, "and the power to make it through the mountains and home."

Roll on, roll on,
Push, push, push,
And finally, back in BRITISH COLUMBIA*!*

When Rick reached the B.C. border, his mother greeted him with a big hug. "Welcome home, son," she said. For a while Rick even forgot how tired and sore he was. He was back in his home province!

In Vancouver, Jack's excitement grew as Rick neared the finish line. Hundreds of children were raising money for Rick—money that would be used for spinal cord research and wheelchair sports. One girl held a slide-a-thon in her backyard. She kept sliding until slide-sickness forced her to stop.

Jack's neighbour Mollie had been helping Rick too. She was a volunteer with the Man in Motion Home Crew.

"It's hard work, but I love it!" she told Jack. "We've been raising money, making travel arrangements, and shipping equipment around the world. The tour is almost over, but there's still lots to do."

Ever since he'd waved goodbye to Rick, Jack had been wondering how he could help. Now he knew!

Vancouver, B.C. | May 23, 1987

Fifty thousand people attended a welcome-home
celebration for the Man in Motion World Tour.
Along with hundreds of other people in wheelchairs,
Jack was given a front row seat.

Rick circled the stadium with an Honour Guard of Canadian wheelchair athletes. He had wheeled more than forty thousand kilometres through thirty-four countries, and now he was crossing the finish line. The applause was tremendous. A magical mood spread through the crowd like a wave.

Rick grinned from ear to ear. He had made it!

When it was over and Rick was leaving, Jack surprised himself by mastering a wheelie.

"Awesome!" said Rick. "You've come a long way, Jack."

"Not as far as YOU, Rick!" Jack beamed. "And guess what? I'm volunteering on weekends with the Home Crew now!"

"Are you?" said Rick. "Great! I'll see you there."

Jack joined the huge crowd leaving the stadium. Everyone was smiling. Jack wasn't the only one who thought Rick was a hero.

The Man in Motion World Tour had proved that people with disabilities could do unbelievably wonderful things— in fact, anything they set their minds to. Jack knew that for Rick, this wasn't the end. It was just the beginning.

Fascinating Facts From The Tour

A Friend Fact

Rick and Terry Fox became friends when they played wheelchair basketball together. Terry died in 1981 after raising awareness and money for cancer research on his cross-Canada Marathon of Hope. His friendship and bravery inspired Rick's Man in Motion World Tour.

Rick carried a small statue of Terry in the motor home. When he felt like giving up, he would look at the statue and remind himself that Terry would never quit. Then he'd get back on the road and push, push, push a little farther.

A Fantastic Fact

Early in the tour, Rick was given an unusual gift—a song! The songwriters had been inspired by a video of Rick wheeling. Although it was really the theme song for a movie, it became the official song of the Man in Motion World Tour.

Rick and his team sang it often. It lifted their spirits and spurred them on. The tune was catchy, and the song became popular around the world.

"Gonna be your man in motion.
All I need is a pair of wheels."

A Figures Fact

During the Man in Motion World Tour:

- 2 birthdays were celebrated by Rick (his 28th and his 29th)
- 4 robberies took place (and none was solved!)
- 94 pairs of wheeling gloves were ruined
- 126 flat tires had to be changed on the motor home
- 160 wheelchair tires wore out
- 730 trips were made to laundromats
- 2,172 postcards were written home
- 40,075 kilometres were wheeled
- And Rick pushed an estimated 10,000,000 strokes!

A Factual Fact PLUS A Fabulous Fact

When Rick was in hospital, physiotherapists taught him exercises and helped him to get up and start wheeling. Later, during his World Tour, Rick worked his body so hard he needed physiotherapy up to three times a day to keep his muscles and joints healthy.

Amanda Reid was Rick's physiotherapist. On the way home, in New Brunswick, Amanda and Rick got engaged. They were married when the tour was over. They live in Richmond, B.C., and have three daughters.

A Final Fact

Rick's Man in Motion World Tour visited 34 countries. The tour took 2 years, 2 months, and 2 days. It raised awareness of what people with disabilities can do. The tour also raised more than $26 million for spinal cord research, rehabilitation, and wheelchair sports.

Dear Readers,

As a young man, I was fortunate to learn a valuable lesson—it's not what happens to you that matters but what you do with it that counts. After my spinal cord injury at the age of fifteen, I was devastated that I had lost the use of my legs. Thanks to the support of people around me, I found the motivation I needed to redefine my goals. In doing so, I realized that the only thing stopping me from achieving my dreams was my own attitude.

Understanding this gave me the confidence to get back into sports, to pursue my dreams, and to ultimately push my wheelchair around the world on my Man in Motion World Tour. I wanted to make a difference in the world, and I knew that if I believed in myself and had the courage to try, anything was possible.

Now it's your turn. You are the leaders of tomorrow—the next generation of Difference Makers. I want to encourage each of you to be powerful champions of change in your own lives. Get involved; contribute; make a difference. I hope my story will inspire your dreams. I truly believe that if enough of us choose to change even one small thing, together we have the power to change anything.

Be positive, and when you meet an obstacle... roll on!

RICK HANSEN

For my grandsons in motion,
Connor and Rowan—roll on! —AM

For Vic, who inspires in the face
of challenge —RL

Greystone Books Ltd.
343 Railway Street, Suite 201
Vancouver BC V6A 1A4
www.greystonebooks.com

Cataloguing data available from Library and Archives Canada
ISBN 978-1-55365-529-9 (cloth)
ISBN 978-1-77100-268-4 (pbk.)
ISBN 978-1-926812-49-6 (ebook)

Editing by Tiffany Stone and Nancy Flight
Copyediting by Shirarose Wilensky
Cover design by Heather Pringle
Cover illustration by Ron Lightburn
Interior design by Setareh Ashrafologhalai
Printed and bound in China by C&C Offset Printing Co., Ltd.
Distributed in the U.S. by Publishers Group West

Song lyrics on page 34 are from
"St. Elmo's Fire (Man in Motion)" by John Parr.

We gratefully acknowledge the financial support of the Canada Council
for the Arts, the British Columbia Arts Council, the Province of British
Columbia through the Book Publishing Tax Credit, and the Government
of Canada through the Canada Book Fund for our publishing activities.

Greystone Books is committed to reducing the consumption of
old-growth forests in the books it publishes. This book is one
step towards that goal.